In the Wild

David Elliott

illustrated by Holly Meade

CANDLEWICK PRESS

First paperback edition 2013

The Library of Congress has cataloged the hardcover edition as follows:
Elliott, David, date.
In the wild / David Elliott ; illustrated by Holly Meade. — 1st ed.
p. cm.
ISBN 978-0-7636-4497-0 (hardcover)
1. Animals—Juvenile poetry. 2. Children's poetry, American. I. Meade, Holly, ill. II. Title.
PS3555.L5674I6 2010
811'.54—dc22 2009008244

ISBN 978-0-7636-6337-7 (paperback)

APS 25 24 23 22 21
15 14 13 12 11 10 9 8

Printed in Humen, Dongguan, China

This book was typeset in Columbus Semi Bold.
The illustrations are woodblock prints and watercolor.

Candlewick Press
99 Dover Street
Somerville, Massachusetts 02144

visit us at www.candlewick.com

To Ester Alexander, the original wild child

D. E.

The Lion

stands alone
on the grassy plain.

He has his pride;
he shakes his mane.

In his eye
the sunset glistens:

when he roars,
the wide world listens.

Big, yet moves
with grace.
Powerful, yet delicate
as lace.

As to color, plain—
an ordinary gray.
But once we start to look,
we cannot look away.

When peaceful, silent;
when angry, loud.

Who would have guessed
the **Elephant**
is so much like a cloud?

The Giraffe

Stilt-walker!
Tree-topper!
Long-necked
show-stopper!

As lovely as the antelope,
as lovely and as fast,
but Antelope
is always first
and **Zebra** always last.

They say that's just the ordered way,
unchangeable, and yet
I wish we had,
for Zebra's sake,
a different alphabet.

A horn stuck on a boot-like face,
So wrong, so clearly out of place.
A frightful sight, preposterous—
it must be a **Rhinoceros**!

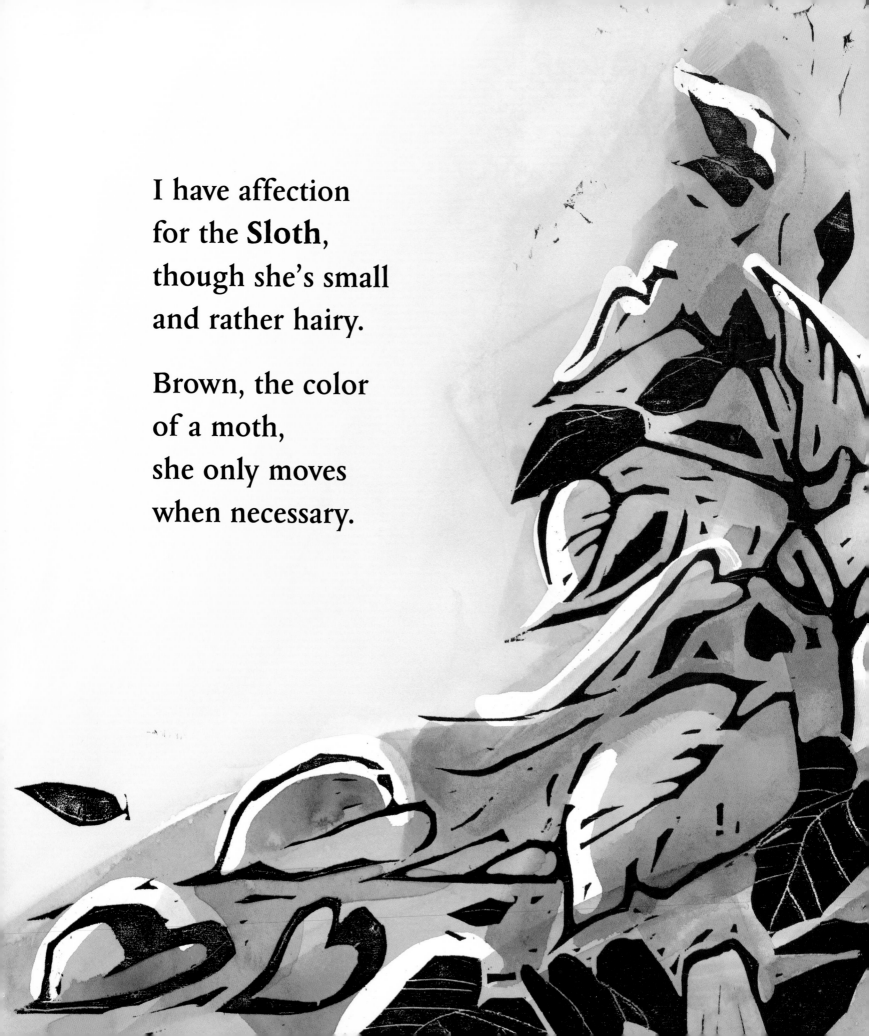

I have affection
for the **Sloth**,
though she's small
and rather hairy.

Brown, the color
of a moth,
she only moves
when necessary.

The **Jaguar**'s back is flowering
with delicate rosettes,
as if she's grown a garden there,
so beautiful, and yet

there's danger in the jaguar's gait,
a soundless step that warns:
Beware of jungle-raised bouquets.
Beware these hidden thorns.

The Panda

You're a bamboo bandit;
you're a piebald dream.
You're a bear in silk pajamas;
you're cookies and cream.
You're the wizard of the mountains;
you're pres-ti-di-gi-ta-tion!
You're nature's best example
of bear imagination.

We can never touch them,
so we love them from afar;
they are wild and distant—
the **Tiger** and the star.

We can never know them;
they are not what we are:
fire, fire, burning bright—
the tiger and the star.

Dear Orangutan,

Three cheers to you, man of the forest.
You arrived here long before us.
You paved the way; you saw it through.
How nice to have someone like you
sitting in our family tree.

Sincerely, from your cousin,
Me

Where are you going,
Kangaroo?
Going going going?
No one can jump
the way you do.
Boing! Boing! Boing!

In burning sun,
in blinding snow,
there stands the mighty **Buffalo**.

His temper short,
his suffering long—
once was sixty-million strong.

In burning sun,
in blinding snow,
behold! The mighty buffalo!

The Wolf

She opens her eyes;
she leaves her lair.
She lifts her head;
she sniffs the air.
And then: *Ahooooo!*

The moon looks down;
a cloud drifts by.
She stands and waits;
there's no reply.
And then: *Ahooooo!*

The Polar Bear

swims

from

floe

to

floe.

Oh!

Look! She's

disappearing . . .

disappearing

in the snow.

If you enjoyed this Candlewick paperback, you and your family are sure to find these books just as delightful!

The powerful jaguar, the beloved panda, and the graceful polar bear are just three of the remarkable creatures in this gorgeous collection of poems and woodcuts.

A companion to *On the Farm,* David Elliott and Holly Meade's celebrated previous collaboration, *In the Wild* is a joyful tribute to favorite creatures around the globe and a wonderful read-aloud to share with young animal lovers.

An American Library Association Notable Children's Book
A New York Public Library 100 Titles for Reading and Sharing Selection
A *Kirkus Reviews* Best Children's Book

★ "A stunning combination of poems and illustrations celebrating some of Earth's wildest and most beautiful creatures."
— *Kirkus Reviews* (starred review)

★ "Meade's woodblock prints . . . have just a hint of humor and capture the powerful wild nature of the creatures. . . . The poems are read-aloud gems."
— *School Library Journal* (starred review)

Ages 4–8
0913

CANDLEWICK PRESS
www.candlewick.com

US $7.99 / $10.99 CAN
ISBN 978-0-7636-6337-7

9 780763 663377

Tops & Bottoms

Adapted and illustrated by
JANET STEVENS

CALDECOTT HONOR BOOK

Scholastic 0-590-86494

SCHOLASTIC